Librarians

By Jacqueline Laks Gorman

Reading consultant: Susan Nations, M.Ed., author/literacy coach/consultant

Gareth Stevens
Publishing

Please visit our Web site www.garethstevens.com. For a free color catalog of all our high-quality books, call toll free 1-800-542-2595 or fax 1-877-542-2596.

Library of Congress Cataloging-in-Publication Data

Gorman, Jacqueline Laks, 1955-
    Librarian / by Jacqueline Laks Gorman.
      p. cm. — (People in my community)
    Summary: A simple introduction to the work of librarians in a library.
    Includes bibliographical references and index.
    ISBN: 978-1-4339-3342-4 (pbk.)
    ISBN: 978-1-4339-3343-1 (6-pack)
    ISBN: 978-1-4339-3341-7 (library binding)
    1. Librarians—Juvenile literature. 2. Libraries—Juvenile literature.
  [1. Librarians. 2. Occupations. 3. Libraries.] I. Title.
  Z682.G68   2002
  020'.23—dc21   2002024199

New edition published 2010 by
Gareth Stevens Publishing
111 East 14th Street, Suite 349
New York, NY 10003

New text and images this edition copyright © 2010 Gareth Stevens Publishing

Original edition published 2003 by Weekly Reader® Books
An imprint of Gareth Stevens Publishing
Original edition text and images copyright © 2003 Gareth Stevens Publishing

Art direction: Haley Harasymiw, Tammy Gruenewald
Page layout: Michael Flynn, Katherine A. Goedheer
Editorial direction: Kerri O'Donnell, Diane Laska Swanke

Cover, back cover, p. 1 © Digital Vision/Getty Images; pp. 5, 7, 11, 15, 17, 19, by Gregg Andersen; pp. 9, 13, 21 © Shutterstock.com.

Printed in the United States of America

CPSIA compliance information: Batch #WW10GS: For further information contact Gareth Stevens, New York, New York at 1-800-542-2595.

Table of Contents

Boldface words appear in the glossary.

Meet the Librarian

A librarian has an important job. A librarian helps people.

A librarian works in the library. A library has many books you can read.

A Librarian's Day

A librarian decides what books to buy for the library.

The librarian puts the books on the **shelves**. Each book has to go in the right place.

shelves

11

Sometimes the librarian uses a computer to answer your questions.

computer

The librarian can help
you find the book
you want.

So Many Books!

The librarian can help you get a **library card**. Then you can take a book home!

library card

The librarian checks out all your books. She tells you when to bring them back.

It looks like fun
to be a librarian!
Would you like to
be a librarian?

Glossary

library card: a special card that is used to check things out of a library

shelves: thin pieces of wood or metal that hold books

For More Information

Books

Ames, Michelle. *Librarians in Our Community.*
New York: PowerKids Press, 2009.

Kirk, Daniel. *Library Mouse.*
New York: Abrams Books for Young Readers, 2007.

Liebman, Dan. *I Want To Be A Librarian.*
Richmond Hill, ON: Firefly Books, 2003.

Monroe, Judy. *A Day in the Life of a Librarian.*
Stevenage, UK: First Fact Books, 2004.

Morris, Ann. *That's Our Librarian!*
Minneapolis, MN: Millbrook Press, 2003.

Web Sites

Community Club: Librarian
http://teacher.scholastic.com/commclub/librarian/index.htm

Index

About the Author

Jacqueline Laks Gorman is a writer and editor. She grew up in New York City and began her career working on encyclopedias and other reference books. Since then, she has worked on many different kinds of books. She lives with her husband and children, Colin and Caitlin, in DeKalb, Illinois.